200

Humorous Sayings About KEY WEST

YOU KNOW YOU LIVE IN KEY WEST WHEN...

PLUS! BONUS SECTION:

Key West Stories, Essays, Articles and Poems

by Major T. Benton

2020

ISBN: 9798667884484
Copyright © 2020 by Major T. Benton
No part of this publication may be reproduced, stored in a retrieval system, or transmitted in any form or by any means – electronic, mechanical, photocopy, recording, or any other.
Book design: Mike Riley, www.ajijicbooks.com
Cover image: Photo unknown
Available on Amazon in Kindle and paperback formats
And from the author directly: majorsigns@aol.com

To J.T. (Jen, Jennifer) O'Lear of Key West.

My dear friend; an incredible Mom to her "Pups"
(as she so graciously referred to her children);
loving heart; talented writer and poet;
generous spirit and deeply beautiful soul.
How fortunate to know you.
Blessed be.

To Jim Simmen, of Key West;

Fellow Vietnam Veteran;
awarded the Silver Star Medal for Gallantry
while receiving two Purple Hearts;
best friend anyone could ever hope for;
exceptional photographer;
author of several books; fisherman; gardener;
environmentalist and ballroom dancer.

Major T Benton

YOU KNOW YOU LIVE IN KEY WEST WHEN...

Contents

You Know You Live in Key West When... Introduction v
②⓪⓪ — COUNT 'EM — things you will recognize right now 1
BONUS SECTION: Key West Stories, Essays, Articles and Poems.......... 37
Essays 39
In The "Briar Patch" with Toni Lynn Washington 40
    At The Green Parrot Bar...40
    Fort Zackery Taylor State Park, Key West, FL...43
Poems - A Selection 45
    Old Blue...46
    Art Related Poems 48
Stories, Articles, & Journal Entries..53
    Divorcing in Key West (Funny... A Little Strange... But True!) 54
    Destination: Fort Jefferson 56
    A Fort, But No Fight..56
    A National Treasure..57
    A Time To Reflect 58
    An Unlikely Departure..58
    Seven On A Raft 59
Dolphin encounters...
    July 1, 1992 – Little Bahama Banks. 60
Reaching The Whales 70
    An Invitation From Pritam Singh 71
    Dr. Payne Discovers A Song 72
    Current Mission Includes Developing Nations 72
    Upgrade To A Full-Blown Research Vessel...73
    Largest Brains On Earth..74
    Changes In Attitudes 74
    Individual Efforts Are Imperative 75
    The Unknown Singh...76
    April 23, 1982: Keys secede from Union, create Conch Republic..........80
A Variety of Additional **Photos** for Your Enjoyment................................83
Epilogue by the Author..97
About the Author 99

You Know You Live In Key West When...

Introduction by the Author – Major T. Benton

The first time I ventured to Key West was during Spring Break in 1979. The Green Parrot Bar was highly recommended to my wife and me for our first beers here. The bartender was as friendly as they come and, after we ordered our "brewskis," he asked where we were from (which was Massachusetts at the time where we were teaching). After he went to pour our drafts, my wife asked me how the bartender knew we weren't from Key West.

The first giveaway was the camera she was wearing around her neck. The second was our flowery, touristy shirts. The third was likely our pale skins from wintering in New England. We were as obvious as any tourists in town.

After the Parrot we walked over to the main drag, Duval Street, where I spotted a somewhat disheveled man standing on the street corner. I had no doubt he was a "local" and, out of curiosity, asked him what it was like to live in Key West. He stood there for a moment, slowly stroking his long goatee, as if giving careful and reasoned consideration to my request.

"Well," he drawled, "Let me put it this way. If you had two heads on your shoulders instead of just one, and walked into any bar in town, the only question someone might ask you would be, 'Would you like a beer...or two?'"

That statement clearly defined the Key West I came to know and love.

With rare exception, Key West lives up to its motto of "One Human Family" where the color of your skin, your religion (whether you have one or not), financial status, nationality, sexual preference(s), age, abilities or disabilities, become insignificant in this most tolerant of towns.

Here, one can be as laid-back and inconspicuous as a sleeping dog in the shade of a mango tree or as active as a nest of unsettled fire ants. The only way Key West might be problematic is if your desire is not to have fun. It's impossible not to do so.

I once had the fascinating pleasure of interviewing Capt. Tony Tarracino, the former Mayor of Key West, whom the New York Times labeled "The Salt of Key West." Tony died in 2008 at the age of 92 and will always be remembered as the owner of Capt. Tony's Saloon, friend and fishing buddy of Ernest Hemingway, gambler, storyteller, gunrunner, shrimper and father of 13 children.

One of my favorite quotes by Capt. Tony is:

Capt. Tony's Saloon has been a favorite hangout for many young musicians looking for a break, which included Jimmy Buffett, long before the

Margaritaville maestro became a household name. Capt. Tony told me the young Buffett often prodded him to let him get up on stage and show what he could do, musically.

"One day, after bugging the hell out of me, I finally agreed and told him, 'OK, here's ten bucks and a six pack. Go do your thing.'"

"Well how did he do?" I asked.

Capt. Tony replied, "Hell, I don't know. I was out front at the time, hitting on a blond, and didn't hear a word of his music." Ha!

Capt. Tony and Jimmy Buffett

However, the two did become fast friends. Buffett, as Campaign Manager, played a role in Capt. Tony's eventual election as Mayor of Key West. Three times before, Capt. Tony had failed. But on his fourth try he won, even if only by 34 votes. Capt. Tony said, "The last time I ran I got several hookers to go and vote for their first time ever. And I won! Ain't that sweet!"

Key West, aka Cayo Hueso (Bone Key), is the oyster within the pearl; the meat with the potatoes; the basics with all the frills; the real thing along with the pretensions.

There is no "status quo" in Key West; no dullness; no saying, "Oh I can't find anything to do." The challenge is deciding which opportunity you want to, or can afford to, pursue. The variety is unending. Enjoy!!!

If you have shared any time in Key West I feel certain you will be able to add many more of your own observations to what you will find in this book. Go for it! If you have never lived in Key West you need to see it for yourself. Welcome!

As those who live here know, humor abounds in Key West in innumerable forms. I hope you enjoy being a part of this insanity within the sanity; this home for whatever your inklings might be. And enjoy these reminders of living in this totally unique environment. Cheers!

You Know You Live In Key West When...

200 — COUNT 'EM — things you will recognize right now that prove you live in Key West, Florida.

Major T Benton

Your coworker has 8 body piercings and none are visible.

You make over $500,000 a year and still can't afford to buy a house.

You have to drive 5 miles per hour down the street behind a tourist trolley "train," which is not an unusual occurrence.

Your child's 3rd-grade teacher has purple hair, a nose ring, and is named "Breeze."

You can't remember... is pot legal?

You've been to baby showers that have two mothers and a sperm donor.

You Know You Live In Key West When

7
For breakfast, you have Cuban bread and Bucci.

8
You know the difference between real and fake Key Lime Pie.

9
A really great parking space can totally move you to tears.

10
The Crime Report is your biggest source of daily entertainment.

11
Gasoline costs more per gallon here than anywhere else in the States with the exception of California.

12
A man walks down the street in full leather regalia and crotch-less chaps, and you hardly even notice.

13
Unlike back home, the lady downtown wearing the baseball cap and sunglasses who looks like Madonna IS Madonna.

14
Your car insurance costs as much as your house payment.

15
Your hairdresser is straight, your plumber is gay, the woman who delivers your mail is into S & M and your Mary Kay representative is a guy in drag.

You know where to find Jimmy Buffett's recording studio.

It's barely sprinkling rain and there's an immediate report on every weather station about a possible "HURRICANE WATCH."

The former owner of your favorite bar was also the former Mayor.

Capt. Tony Tarracino for Mayor

When the temperature drops to 60 degrees, you break out the socks and sweaters, or turn on the oven and leave the oven door open.

Both you AND your cat have therapists.

The smelly, shoeless, shirtless, alcoholic bum hitting you up for money has to interrupt his begging to answer the cell phone in the back pocket of his torn jean shorts.

It's perfectly normal for a 50-year-old lawyer to try cases in court during the day and chase 17-year-olds at night.

The coldest temperature ever recorded is 41 and the record high is 97.

You step outside at night, say "Here kitty, kitty," and 137 cats show up.

You go to retrieve your big, green trash container from the curb a few hours after trash pickup and find 17 plastic bags of discarded dog crap already fermenting inside.

A pack of cigarettes costs up to $8.00 depending on where you buy them in town.

Major T Benton

The only pressure you experience is the water pressure, and even that's pretty low.

A man with two heads on his shoulders, instead of just one, can walk into any bar along Duval Street and the only thing anyone might say to him is, "You want a beer...or two?"

You call yourself multilingual because you are able to swear at people in their native language.

KEY WEST CHICKEN FAMILY

The hottest topic of discussion in town is what to do about all the chickens running around.

You Know You Live In Key West When

You get your makeup tips from a local drag queen.

FIVE QUEENS IN KEY WEST

The pilot of the little plane you are about to go up in for your first ever skydive, and who is dressed in shorts, a t-shirt and flip-flops, says to you, "People ask me why anyone would want to jump out of a perfectly good airplane? Well, this is NOT a perfectly good airplane."

(3)(3)

The highlight of the 87-year-old former Mayor's birthday party was the nude appearance of his favorite stripper who had shaved her beaver into the shape of a heart, just for him.

You walk past a guy wearing a Pirate's outfit who has a baby attached to his shoulder dressed as a parrot - a real baby.

35

The silver statue atop a pedestal on the street corner says "Thank you" when you put a dollar in her outstretched hand.

36

Your favorite T-shirt is emblazoned with: "Save the Bales."

37

Your daughter is named Wilhemina. Your son, Anthony, is affectionately called "Capt. Tony," and at least one of your cats is named Margarita.

38

You've stood on the spot where Hemingway used to box, which just happens to be next to what used to be a bordello.

39

Everyplace else you ever lived, you always felt you didn't fit in and were different from everyone else. But here, everyone is different, so you fit in perfectly.

40

When you walk behind someone with a long ponytail and loop earrings, it's often a man. If the person has short hair, a buzz cut and eight studs in each ear, it's usually a woman.

41

The people camping out in the mangroves next to the beach are not Boy Scouts.

42

You get paid on Friday afternoon, go a local Bar for happy hour, pay back everyone you borrowed money from the previous week, buy a couple of rounds of beers and shots for your buddies, and are borrowing money again before you leave.

You Know You Live In Key West When

Each June, at the beginning of hurricane season, you take bets on which of the stores that close for the summer will actually reopen again in the fall.

Each week you go to 1-2 parties for friends who are moving back "up north" and 1-2 parties for friends who have returned from "up north," at least one of whom you've welcomed back twice before.

The restaurant owner is French, the manager is Latino, the hostess is Mexican, the bartender is Danish, the waiter is from Senegal, and the chef is Polish.

You meet a couple in their eighties from Ohio who look like everyone's favorite Grandmother and Grandfather. They're hobbling down the street, arm in arm, broadly smiling and wearing brand new T-shirts. Hers reads "I'm A Lean, Mean Farting Machine," and his proclaims "Show Me Your Hooters!"

There's only one way in and out of here, over 43 bridges covering 129 miles to and from mainland Florida.

You have friends who, for over twenty years, have moved back to Pittsburgh every few years to earn enough money to come back and live here again.

During the summer, condensation forms on your butt from the warm water in the toilet bowl.

Following the Fantasy Fest parade, a nude woman, body-painted to look like a tiger, yells your name and throws her arms around your neck. You discover she is one of your students from the local college.

You ride the Conch Train and are shocked at two people carrying on a conversation in English.

Your six o'clock shadow is just a cruise ship blocking the sunset.

You're told a hurricane is coming and you should stock up on canned goods, so you go out and buy three cases of beer.

Guys who are bald on top still wear ponytails.

TIGER WOMAN

You walk into any bar in town more than once and your drink of choice is placed in front of you before you even have a chance to say "Hi" to the bartender.

Seeing a car shaped and painted like a chili pepper or another one covered in pieces of glass and jewels is considered normal.

The guy with the trained house cats that jump through rings of fire at sunset is your neighbor.

The woman selling cookies from her bicycle each evening is also your art teacher and masseuse.

The bitch sitting next to you at the bar is a real dog; a female canine, as in Rat Terrier.

Tourists go ballistic when they see "dolphin" (as in "mahi-mahi" or "dorado") listed on the seafood restaurant menu. Could it be Flipper?

You still can't remember... Is pot legal?

The dinner party wine is served in plastic cups.

A guy sees his picture in the paper hugging a beautiful woman sitting in his lap from a party the night before; only to later learn "she" was a "he."

You never judge a man until you have walked a mile in his red pumps.

You drop your wallet and, fearful of bending over to pick it up, you kick it all the way home.

SPRING BREAKERS

The best game of dominoes is during Spring Break when one drunken college kid stumbles and knocks over several others.

A two-bedroom, one-bath "neighborhood" home described as the "perfect place to raise a family" is listed for $999,000.

A "classic" two-bedroom, one-bath Conch house in Bahama Village, with "excellent renovation potential" is listed for $899,000.

The 50 ft. wide property, with a one-story, on-its-last-legs, "shotgun" house and tiny yard filled with "debris," is situated between two, mammoth, three-story elegant homes with widow walks and orchid-laced, jungle-like landscaping.

You Know You Live In Key West When

A "category five" hangover means you are afraid you are not going to die.

Tourists want to overachieve and locals want to underachieve.

GREEN PARROT CRAZY TIMES

Your bartender used to be a doctor in International Falls, Minnesota.

Nightly worship services are held throughout town at the altar of our Lord Jagermeister.

There are more churches per capita than any other city in the United States. Contrarily, there also happen to be more bars per capita than any other city in the U.S. Think there's some correlation here?

Major T Benton

Your bartender is basically a pharmacist with unlimited choices to fill your prescription.

Spring Breakers arrive on vacation and leave on probation.

The city's unofficial motto is "A Work Free Drug Place."

You're told you live in the last bastion of the overqualified.

It's O.K. to grow old disgracefully.

A crime is committed and the police round up the unusual suspects.

The official yard ornament status symbols are the port-a-potty and construction dumpster.

The most popular and often seen sets of "luggage" around town are the ubiquitous plastic grocery bags.

You've seen many a cat on the hot tin roof of Tennessee Williams' house.

You ignore a homeless person begging for money and she screams at you, calling you a hobophobiac!

You Know You Live In Key West When

A, AA, AAA, C and D are the only alphabet you need during hurricane season.

When friends stop by, you use your washing machine as a cooler, filling it with ice and beer for the evening's refreshments.

Bicycles on the Beach

Your bicycle is stolen (again) and the thief leaves you your helmet.

Your bicycle seat is stolen (again) so you decide to ride standing from now on.

Major T Benton

Your front wheel is stolen from your bicycle (again), so you decide to become a unicyclist.

It's your God given right to sit on your front steps in your underwear and eat Chinese take-out by candlelight.

Downed power lines make excellent security systems.

(9)(2)
Air Conditioning wins hands-down as the best invention ever.

You're living in the only frost-free city in the continental United States.

(9)(4)
No matter how hard the hurricane winds blow, roadside campaign signs still survive.

Two can live as cheaply as one, but only for half as long as anyplace else.

The "FREE BEER TOMORROW" sign outside a local bar has kept you returning, and parched, for over a week until you finally figure "It ain't going to happen."

The high cost of living here hasn't affected its popularity.

You Know You Live In Key West When

Anyone with an opinion, no matter how stupid, gets published in the Citizen's Voice page of the daily paper.

One of the most historical downtown theater buildings becomes a Walgreens drug store.

The longest, most costly, most publicized court trial is held to determine the legal owner of "Bigfoot" the 7-toed cat.

You learn the difference between French Canadians and canoes is that canoes tip.

RIDING SCOOTERS IN KEY WEST

You see hordes of adult tourists recklessly racing scooters up and down the main drag, incessantly beeping their little horns and shouting "Wa-hoo!"

1 0 3
The woman hawking cigars in the temporary booth during the day waits tables at dinnertime and is a stripper at "Teasers" at night.

CONCH REPUBLIC FLAG

1 0 4
The most popular beaches are sometimes posted with signs warning of "Fecal Contamination."

1 0 5
Fresh-water Conchs (locals who have lived here for 7 years or more) wax nostalgically about the memorable stench of urine that perpetually emanated from the now demolished Red's Place on Caroline Street.

You Know You Live In Key West When

106
You can have your lunch in a restaurant while in the nude, and while waited on by topless servers.

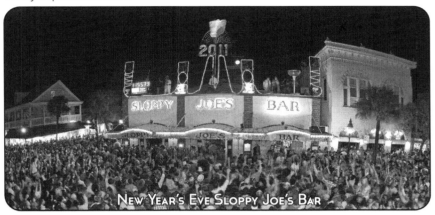

107
A city commissioner, with explosives, straps himself to a tree and threatens to blow himself up to keep some federal property from being developed into condos.

108
The population of 26,000 soars to 75,000 in the last week of October for Fantasy Fest weekend.

109
All you have to do to keep employed is show up, preferably sober, or even better, show up sober AND on time.

110
The city's proud motto is "One Human Family."

111
You put more miles on your shoes and bike than you do your car.

Major T Benton

(1)(1)(2)
The main drag, Duval Street, is the longest street in the world (metaphorically speaking), running from the Atlantic Ocean to the Gulf of Mexico.

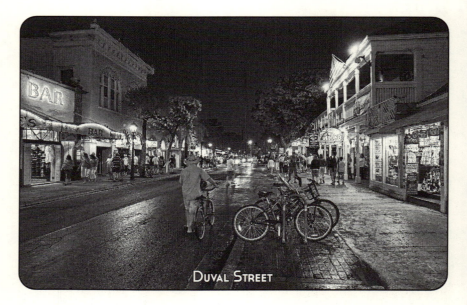
DUVAL STREET

(1)(1)(3)
You live at the end of the road, Mile Zero of U.S. Rt.1; the end of the rainbow; in a place sometimes better known as Key Wasted or Key Weird.

(1)(1)(4)
Your water comes from a pipe that travels 130 miles from the mainland.

(1)(1)(5)
You've seceded where others failed.

(1)(1)(6)
You're invited to a social event but explain you're writing, or painting, or some other activity, and the caller totally understands your need for

creative time and space and will you call back another time.

You live closer to Havana, Cuba, than you do to Miami.

The only closet in your house is a $21.99 plastic tent from Wal-Mart, which also means you have to remove hanging clothes from the shower rod every time you want to take a shower.

You see a grave marker in the local cemetery that reads: "I Told You I Was Sick."

On New Year's Eve, at midnight you have to choose between watching a giant conch shell lowered from the top of a bar; or, a drag queen lowered in an enormous, red high-heeled shoe from the roof of another bar; or a "wench" lowered from the boom of a sailing ship in the harbor.

NEW YEAR'S EVE RED SLIPPER

You are able to pay your rent by the extra money you make hand-painting-boobs and bodies during Fantasy Fest.

PAINTED BODIES AT FANTASY FEST

(1)(2)(2)
People stop what they're doing, including talking, to observe, clap and cheer as the sun sets each evening.

(1)(2)(3)
The phone book has a hurricane-tracking map just inside the cover.

(1)(2)(4)
You know it's July because there are a gazillion Hemingway look-alikes in town for their annual festival.

(1)(2)(5)
You go to a drag race and actually see drag queens racing down the street in their very high heels.

① ② ⑥
You like your vice, versa.

① ② ⑦
You ask your neighbors why they're all here and they tell you it's because they're not all there!

① ② ⑧
Your city is referred to as "An open-air nut factory with a liquor license."

① ② ⑨
You see store signs stating, "Sorry, We're Open."

① ③ ⓪
Hurricanes are immediately followed by T-shirts which read, "I Was Blown by Hurricane (fill in the blank)."

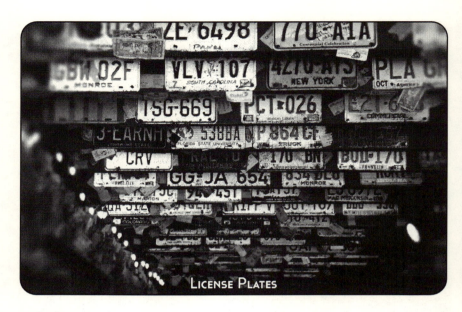

LICENSE PLATES

①③①
You buy amazingly fresh shrimp and cocktail sauce by the gallon.

①③②
The music group for the evening is named "Big Dick and the Extenders."

①③③
You live in a place that has no dignity, but a lot of style.

①③④
Once you have ruined your reputation you can live the way you want.

①③⑤
The majority of the residents are dreamers, drifters, dropouts, barflies, writers, artists, treasure hunters, gays, real estate speculators, smugglers, pensioners, runaways and fishermen.

You Know You Live In Key West When

A county prosecutor is arrested after running naked across the parking lot of a local motel and jumping into the back seat of an occupied car he mistook for a friend's.

You are still using the paper license tag that came with your car five years ago.

Your favorite restaurant has an enchilada list instead of a wine list.

You buy your booze and do your banking at a drive-up window.

You have license plates on your wall, but not on your car.

Most restaurants you go to begin with "El."

You hated New Yorkers until those worst drivers in the world from Quebec started coming down.

The tires holding down the shingles on your roof have more tread on them than the ones on your car.

You price-shop for shrimp.

(145) You think a red light at an intersection is merely a suggestion.

(146) You believe using a turn signal is a sign of weakness.

(147) You think six tons of crushed rock makes a beautiful front lawn.

(148) You ran for state legislature so you can speed legally.

(149) You pass on the right because that's the fast lane.

(150) You read a book while driving from home to Miami and back.

(151) You use aluminum foil and duct tape to repair your air conditioner.

(152) There is a piece of a UFO displayed in your home.

(153) You wish you had invested in portable toilets.

(154) Your satellite dish got knocked off your roof by a waterspout.

You Know You Live In Key West When

You've been on TV more than three times telling about how the chickens keep you awake at night or about your alien abductions.

You've heard there is a place called Tallahassee in the northwestern part of the state above you.

You wash your jeans to "dress up" and go to Miami.

Your other vehicle is also a bicycle.

Two of your cousins are in Tallahassee—one in the legislature and the other in the state pen.

Your car is missing a fender or bumper.

You're relieved when the pavement ends because the dirt road has fewer potholes.

You can correctly pronounce Felice, Cayo Hueso, Chicharrones, Mesón, and Siboney.

At a Fantasy Fest celebration in your favorite bar, the bra on the girl in the middle of the dance floor is constructed entirely of glued-on Cheerios, which, one-by-one, as she gyrates, begin flying through the air, and you've never seen so many cereal lovers in your life.

You see nothing odd when, in the conversations of the people in line around you at the grocery store, every other word alternates between Spanish and English, with a dash of Spanglish thrown in.

One of your favorite restaurants has a graveyard in it.

You associate Key West with places to make your last stand. On April 23, 1982, the Keys seceded from the Union and created the "Conch Republic." To this day the Conch Republic issues its own passports and every year, during the week of April 23, there is an Independence Day celebration marking the birth of the first "sovereign state of mind."

You still can't remember... Is pot legal?

You have been told by at least one out-of-state vendor that they are going to charge you extra for "international" shipping, and that makes you extremely proud.

Your city is referred to as "the end of the road" and the biggest cul-de-sac in existence.

Your first job here was working as a prep cook at a restaurant called "The Ugly Rooster."

Your city is known as "A Drinking Town with a Tourist Problem."

You Know You Live In Key West When

1 7 2
Your city is also known as a "Work Free Drug Place."

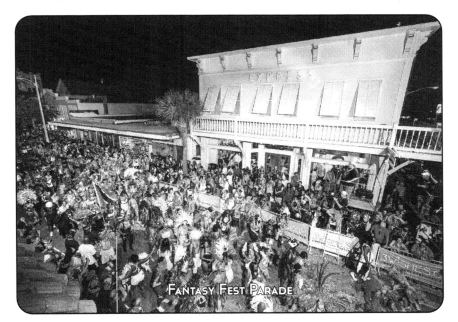

1 7 3
Your city has a pink submarine.

1 7 4
The biggest thing in common between the local citizens and the shrimp in the offshore waters is they both only come out at night.

1 7 5
You find out a "gentleman" named Count von Cosel from Germany once lived in your city and was so obsessed with a young lady that when she died, he removed her dead body from the cemetery and slept with her in his bed for seven years before being found out.

Major T Benton

Some of your residents and long-term visitors include Ernest Hemingway, Shel Silverstein, Harry Truman, Tennessee Williams, Robert Frost, Thomas A. Edison, Jimmy Buffett, Capt. Tony Tarracino, Richard Wilbur, Elizabeth Bishop, Annie Dillard, John Hersey, Alison Lurie, James Merrill, Wallace Stevens, Philip Caputo, John Dewey, Hunter S. Thompson, Judy Bloom and a fire chief named Bum Farto.

The garbage trucks have "We Cater Weddings" painted on their sides.

There is a tombstone in the cemetery with the words, "Now I Know Where You Are Sleeping," put there by this gentleman's wife.

Written on a local bar's bathroom wall can be found the deeply philosophical statement, "I'd Rather Have a Bottle in Front of Me than a Frontal Lobotomy."

Everyone living here is tuned a little off-key.

Your favorite bar is referred to as "A Sunny Place for Shady People," "Where Birds of all Feathers Flock Together;" and where signs are posted saying, "No Cover. No Minimum. No Wonder;" and "The Management is Not Responsible - Period."

The motto of your favorite bar, the Green Parrot, is "No Snivelling," and perhaps the green condoms sold in their gift shop should read, "No Shrivelling," but that's another story.

You discover that a gazillion termites, holding hands, are the only reason your house is still standing.

You can't see the house across the street from you because it is blocked from view by the gigantic satellite dish on the front lawn.

The motto of students on Spring Break is "See the Lower Keys on your Hands and Knees."

GREEN PARROT BAR

1 8 6
All the bicycles parked outside the bars are not there because the customers inside are environmentally friendly patrons. It's because they've lost their driver's licenses from driving under the influence.

(1)(8)(7)
You got a DUI while peddling your bicycle home from your favorite bar.

(1)(8)(8)
At Sunset Celebration on Mallory dock, the street entertainer, swaying precariously in the middle of the tightrope wire, ten feet above the cement and, while holding three tennis balls in his hands, yells out, "Now watch carefully as I juggle all five balls!

(1)(8)(9)
You are now living in your fourth rental in three years because the places you had lived in before were sold to new home buyers.

(1)(9)(0)
You luck out one night when a flatbed truck is surreptitiously parked in front of Jimmy Buffett's Margaritaville restaurant. Buffett himself jumps onto this makeshift stage for an unannounced appearance and for two hours sings most of your favorites.

You Know You Live In Key West When

① ⑨ ①
The world's longest Gay Pride flag is unfurled by 2,000 volunteers, reaching from the Atlantic Ocean end of Duval Street, along the 14 blocks to the other end of Duval, reaching 1.25 miles to the Gulf of Mexico.

① ⑨ ②
You work for an environmental education foundation located on a tiny island near Key West and a float plane lands with Jimmy Buffett as the pilot. After asking about the programs and checking out the island, Jimmy departs. Two weeks later the Foundation receives an unsolicited $10,000 check from Buffett in support of your programs.

1 9 3
You can visit Fort Jefferson in the Dry Tortugas National Park, 68 miles (109 km) west of Key West where Dr. Samuel Mudd, an American physician, was imprisoned for treeating the broken leg of John Wilkes Booth who had just assassinated President Abraham Lincoln.

1 9 4
Your conservative sister and her hubby from Virginia visit -- but refuse to go to the La te Da night club for a show put on by amazingly talented female impersonators. However, when your 22-year-old son visits, he doesn't hesitate and ends up rolling in the aisles with appreciation and laughter.

1 9 5
The reservations manager at a local hotel has a sign in her office that reads, "It's not PMS. I'm always a bitch!"

1 9 6
You have a bad accident and are taken to the Hospital's emergency room only to learn the doctor on call is your drinking and pool-shooting buddy; yet you never even knew he was a doctor.

1 9 7
You visit friends and they introduce you to "Art," a 3-foot long Iguana purchased at the weekly flea market on Big Pine Key. Why the name, "Art?" "Well," your buddy explains, "My wife and her sister went to the flea market to buy 'Art,' and this is what they brought home."

1 9 8
You spend an hour searching for the "No Name Pub," on "No Name Key," about 30 minutes north of Key West. The pub describes itself as "A NICE PLACE if you can find it." You find it, and it is!

On the return flight to Key West from Fort Jefferson and the Dry Tortugas National Park, you are seated behind a stinky, sunburned, handcuffed man who had just been arrested for stealing a Jet Ski in Key West and trying to ride it to Cuba!

And last, but not least: YOU KNOW YOU LIVE IN KEY WEST WHEN...

Major T Benton

BONUS SECTION

Key West Stories, Essays, Articles and Poems

Major T Benton

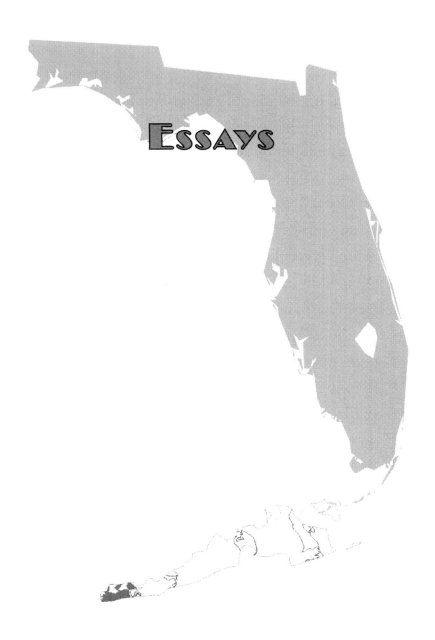

Essays

In The "Briar Patch" With Toni Lynn Washington

At The Green Parrot Bar

In Key West, Florida, 2004

As Brer Rabbit said to Brer Fox, "I don't keer w'at you do wid me, Brer Fox," sezee, . . . "hang me des ez high as you please . . . drown me des ez deep ez you please... skin me, snatch out my eyeballs, . . . but please, please, don't fling me in dat briar patch." – *Joel Chandler Harris*

Teacher: "One suggestion for your assignment is to go to the Green Parrot Bar this weekend and check out a great blues singer, Toni Lynn Washington."

Student: "Oh no! Not the Green Parrot briar patch! Please, please, I'll go anywhere, do anything, but don't make me go to the Parrot!"

Today, the Green Parrot Bar in Key West is, in fact, a "briar-patch," a safe haven for many who wish to escape from the stresses and travails of life in the "real world," even if only for a few minutes or hours. What draws many local patrons and tourists alike, is the sense of community found at this "Southernmost Center for Culture"—well, "maybe not for the cultural elite, but certainly for the culturally deprived." The Parrot is affectionately referred to as "A Sunny Place for Shady People . . . where birds of all feathers flock together . . . keeping the men and women of Key West well-lubricated since 1890."

The Parrot also claims to be "the home of great drinks and bad art" where there is never a cover charge for the entertainment. "No Cover. No Minimum. No Wonder." The art? Well, yes, I'm sure art critics would proclaim it as "bad," particularly the paintings of Einstein and of "Smirk" (a local served as the model), which now appear on Green Parrot "parrotphenalia." But it's impossible to look at these and the other "works of art" holding up the aged, termite-ridden walls without smiling and being reminded of some good time had by all. How can anyone argue with the bar's motto, "No Sniveling," or the sign, "The Management is Not Responsible," period. (An aside: On the packages of green condoms sold in their gift shop, I suggested they stamp the message "No Shriveling!"

What's makes the Green Parrot so successful? It's the camaraderie, the entertainment, and primarily the music of the Blues holding it all together, as exemplified by the performance of Toni Lynn Washington. For over 40 years, Ms. Washington has been singing the blues, traveling throughout Europe, Canada and the United States, having begun her journey learning the gospel songs in her native Southern Pines, North Carolina. Although she began her first set Friday night with a rocking interpretation of the Hank Williams classic, "Hey, Hey Good Looking," Toni says she has been most heavily influenced by such Blues greats as Ruth Brown, Ma Rainey, Joe Williams, John Lee Hooker and Bessie Smith.

The songs kept coming, each one building on the other. Everyone could feel the crescendo slowly rising as she mastered the phrases, giving her sultry, soulful take on "Unchain My Heart," "I Got To Know," and "I Only Have Eyes For You." She peaked with the last number of the set, bringing this diverse audience – of carpenters and wealthy tourists, conch train drivers and nurses, the elite and the downtrodden, the old and young – to its feet, dancing, clapping, singing along with her as her entire body shook with the sexually suggestive "Rock Me Baby, Rock Me All Night Long."

During the break, I asked a bartender, several patrons, and Toni Lynn Washington, herself, to describe their take on the Blues. The bartender told me he has been working here five years and what makes him look forward to coming to work each day is the sense of community and family he feels here. He said, "The Blues is a put-your-hands-together-and-join-in kind of feeling where everyone, no matter what their current status in life may be, can find happiness within the loneliness, and feel like something larger than their individual selves."

Various customers described the Blues as "like getting lost for a while;" "the Blues makes me emote;" "in all its sadness, the feeling of community makes life bearable;" "somehow, when I'm listening, I know hope is on the way;" and, perhaps most succinctly said, "the blues is talking about real shit."

Toni Lynn sat quietly at the edge of the stage, selling her CD's and chatting with the patrons. How does someone 67-years of age find community while traveling 45-50 weeks a year? To her, the audience is her adopted family, so wherever she goes, she always feels at home. She returns to the Green Parrot because she loves the great people who work at and frequent the place, and because she always gets a great reception here. She was once married and has grown children living in Louisiana and Massachusetts. She most cherishes the holidays and the two weeks each year when they all get together in Boston.

My strongest impression of Toni Lynn Washington is stated in the title of her CD, Born to Sing. In my final conversation with her, she summed up her feelings about the blues, and what this music means to her, with one word – "Work!" And after a good laugh, she told me, "I guess misery really does just likes company."

The patrons at the Green Parrot would undoubtedly agree. When they arrive, they leave their miseries outside and throw themselves into the most comforting briar-patch around.

In The "Briar Patch" with Toni Lynn Washington

Fort Zackery Taylor State Park, Key West, FL
February 20, 2005

At the southern edge of Key West, Fort Zackery Taylor predates the Civil War and is a National Historic Monument. Beyond its historical importance, the park is the southernmost state park in the continental United States.

Fort Zack. I've been there so many, many times; to relax, write, paint, ponder, grieve, walk, bike, picnic, swim, sun, meet friends, attend a variety of events, and sometimes just to lose myself so I could find myself again. But I had never really looked at the water; the ocean and the gulf, and where the two merge. I'd just taken it for granted all these years.

Today I carefully observed the waters off Fort Zack, from looking at them from a distance through the canon portholes of the Fort itself, to getting into it physically, immersing myself within. I touched it, smelled it, tasted it, listened to it, consciously looked at it, and let it be itself.

I thought about water being a finite substance. There's only so much – always has been – the same amount of water since our planet was formed, cycled over and over and over.

I thought about how the salty drops clinging to my beard could contain the very molecules of the rain that fell on the Pyramids in Egypt thousands of years ago, or perhaps from the iceberg that sunk the Titanic. Water from Thoreau's Walden Pond could have evaporated and become part of a cloud that found its way to the Keys.

Talk about cycles! Talk about living and dying and living again. Talk about the Phoenix rising from the ashes every 600 years. When you think about water, you think about power, life, value, birth, vastness, necessity, magnitude and vitality – the basic element of all life. 70% of our own bodies are this very substance.

I looked closely for color this day and was rewarded with surprising diversity. Different colors when the sun was unrestricted than when heavily shrouded by cumulus clouds, or than when the UV rays came through thin clouds of the cirrus variety. Different colors when the wind blew, when the shadow of a pelican crossed it, when a jet ski skimmed its surface or a sailing vessel cut through its resistance creating prisms of light in the mist of the spray, producing miniature rainbows only a few feet high and not much more in length.

As the current moved and changed direction with the tide and the winds,

I thought about the life within these waters and how there's so much we don't know about our oceans. It made me think how I hope we never know all there is to know about anything, because it's better being part of the mystery and feeling alive. As Joseph Campbell wrote, "We are that mystery we are seeking to find."

Painting of Ocean Waters off Fort Zack

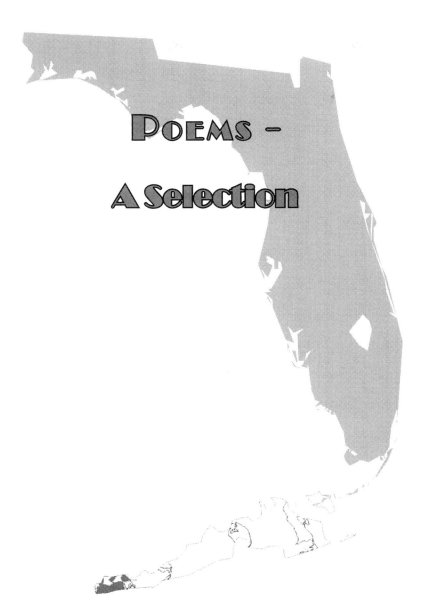

Poems –
A Selection

Old Blue

He didn't start out
With this moniker
But he earned it.
Especially the "old" part,
And he's proud.

An immigrant from Germany,
Old Blue came here by ship in 1969.
From Baltimore he ventured forth,
Heading west to the lure
Of California and home in Riverside.

Old Blue traversed the Pacific coast,

From Baja in Mexico to Puget Sound.
He was popular in Vancouver,
Tested hard in Yosemite's mountains
And the torrid expanses of the Mojave.

After seventeen years out west,
Old Blue headed back
To his coast of entry,
Settling this time
As a pilgrim in Massachusetts.

For eighteen more years
Old Blue has duplicated
His West Coast successes,
From Nova Scotia and Maine
To the end of the road in Key West.

For thirty-five years he's served me well,
As faithful as any friend could be.
He's heard my grievances and incantations,
Reverberated with my joys and ecstasies.
And been there when I needed him most.

For 368,000 miles,
(14 times around the world!)
And still purring along,
He's proud to be A 69 VW Kombi van.
Old Blue.

An Update as of 2020

Old Blue and I now reside in Ajijic (pronounced "Ah-hee-heek"), a small town in the state of Jalisco, México. Now fifty years of age, Old Blue has well over 400,000 miles on his odometer (more than 15 times around the world) and is still running strong. Lucky me to have such a loyal friend!

Old Blue and the Old Man

Art Related Poems

NOTE From the Author: When I lived in Key West I had the amazing good fortune to have two exceptional art teachers whom I will always revere. The first was the now deceased Joachim (Joe) K. Loeber, an artist of great international accomplishments over a long life that spanned the years from his birth in Germany, to living in other parts of Europe, and, eventually moving to America -- including more than 35 years in Key West. For a concise coverage of Joe Loeber's life, go to www.goleader.com/13nov14/12.pdf.

The classes Joe presented in his studio, limited to six students, were so much fun! He never said, "Here's a bowl of fruit. Now paint it and then I will critique your work." No, never. But with the energy, excitement and enthusiasm of a 16-year-old, his classes were about experimenting with as many of the materials and techniques of painting as we could possibly imagine. "Oh, look at this! What fascinating use of blending colors she's displaying here." Or, "Check this out! He's designing a work of art by spreading the paint with a plastic credit card!"

Art critic, Stephen Langford, wrote: "Loeber's versatility is such that to list his favorite themes would sound like an index to an art encyclopedia. He has no style, so varied and brilliant is each work."

My other teacher was Roberta B. Marks. Roberta is a much-celebrated and loved Key West artist who works in sculpture, mixed-media, painting, constructions and collage. She has shown in galleries and museums throughout the United States and abroad, including the Smithsonian Institution and the Victoria and Albert Museum in London. She has lectured in University settings here and in Europe, and is represented in Key West by the Lucky Street Gallery. For more information on Roberta Marks, go to www.robertabmarks.com.

I was a student in several of Roberta's classes at the College of the Florida Keys. The classes met for three hours, once a week. The most powerful and influential times were the first 30 minutes +/-, when Roberta was able to put

Art Related Poems

the class into a relaxed "spell" as she discussed her Zen Buddhism and how it influenced her art and her life. It was a truly mesmerizing experience.

When enrolled in her class on "Abstract Art," I well remember the day I walked into the room and said to Roberta, "I shouldn't even be here today. The last 24 hours have been so chaotic I don't think I can paint a thing!" To which she replied, "Paint chaos! Paint chaos!

And "paint chaos" I did. Not only was it incredibly cathartic, but it also turned into a piece that quickly sold at the gallery where it was placed.

The following is a two-part poem I wrote related to being in Roberta's classes.

Out of Your Head

"Make yourself vulnerable," she said.
"You want to paint vases,
Pretty flowers,
Bowls of fruit?
You're in the wrong class.

"This is abstract art.
This is going inside yourself.
This is about emotional energy
Stored within you,
Needing to get out.

"A very physical task here,
Letting go!
Releasing!
Expanding your awareness!
Getting out of your head!

"Abstract painting is not accessible.
It takes excavation,
Remaining in a vulnerable state.
It's a path to discover
Who you are.

"It must jolt you
And make you feel,

Feel possessed and out of control.
Open up!
Allow the healing to begin.

"It's not what you 'see,'
But what you
Make
To be
Seen.

"You'll make visible
What,
Without you,
Would never
Have been visible.

"Release.
Let go!
Make the brush an extension
Of your fingers, hand, arm,
Heart and soul.

"Free yourself
Of the pain,
The fear,
The guilt.
Relax.

"And when you've exhausted
The possibilities,
And shut nothing out,
You may not
Have all the answers.

"But you will
Keep asking
All
The right
Questions."

Out of My Head

Letting go.
Releasing.
Freeing myself.
It all sounds
So easy.

It even sounds
Like fun.
Exhaling.
Getting out
The 'Nam' demons.

How can anything
Be so deeply hidden
Within oneself
That getting it out
Seems impossible?

Everyone
Has a skeleton
In the closet.
Why would mine
Be any different?

How do I get to
That empty, non-thinking
Zero zone,
Foregoing intellect,
And going with emotion?

If being locked
In a padded room,
Or getting shock treatments,
Would get me 'out of my head,'
I'd volunteer.

The blessing
Is the desire
To keep attempting,
The hope to overcome,
The dream of peace within.

If I can
View the parts
With compassion,
I can understand
The whole.

If I will allow
And not
Force,
I will empty
And fill.

If I can stay
At the center
Of my being
I will
Learn.

If I can keep
The course,
Eventually,
All
Will flow.

Stories, Articles, & Journal Entries

Divorcing in Key West

(Funny... A Little Strange... But True!)

MY first wife and I were married for 25+years. Since our divorce in 1993, and to this day, we remain very supportive of each other, the best of friends, and sharing in the lives of our son, daughter-in-law, granddaughter and mutual friends.

When it became time for us to embark on separate paths my wife was living in New York and I was living in Grassy Key, just north of Marathon in the Florida Keys. For a variety of reasons, it was simpler to file for divorce in Florida.

I called the judge's office in Marathon, set up the divorce proceedings date for the upcoming Thursday - the day before my wife was scheduled to fly back to New York from Key West - and asked for any pertinent instructions we might need to know in order to appear before the judge. They sent me a copy of the court protocols. Everything seemed set. But, then again, this was the Florida Keys! "You want it when!!??"

The day before our scheduled divorce hearing, the assistant to the judge in Marathon called with an unusual request. Our divorce case was the only case scheduled on the Judge's docket that Thursday and the judge wanted to go fishing. I'm not joking! Then the assistant told me that a judge in Key West had an opening for the following day, on Friday morning, if that was okay with us.

Since my wife was scheduled to fly out of Key West later that Friday afternoon, we agreed. On Friday morning we left Grassy Key very early, with much appreciation to "Old Blue," my 1969 VW Kombi, so we could make the hour's drive to Key West with plenty of time to be at the Judge's Chambers by 10 A.M. No problems there. However, when we arrived at the courthouse we received some disturbing news. The receptionist at the entrance to the Judge's Chambers informed me I could not "present myself" before the judge since I was dressed in Bermuda shorts. I explained to the receptionist I had received information from the Court in Marathon about all the requirements for appearance before the judge and there was never any mention of needing to be in long pants!

The receptionist informed me that the rules and regulations for the Marathon court were different from the rules and regulations for the Key West court. What? I was furious! When the assistant calmly informed me we would have to come back another day, I exclaimed, "But we can't come back another day! My wife has a flight this afternoon to return to New York!"

My wife was similarly upset but assuredly told me she had an idea. She told the receptionist we would return shortly. We went out to the street where "Old Blue" was parked. I opened the sliding, side door so my wife could retrieve her suitcase. Inside she located a pair of her khaki pants that had an easily expandable elastic waistband.

I stepped inside Old Blue, removed my Bermuda shorts, and pulled on the khakis. I could get them around my waist okay but they were ridiculously short in length. However, what choice did I have?

Just before entering the Judge's Chambers I pulled the pants legs down as far as possible. I could "present myself" to enter, and enter we did. It only took about 15 minutes for the judge to finalize our divorce settlement.

I can't imagine a simpler divorce than ours. The total cost for all the proceedings was something like $89.00! We had divided everything equally; had no disagreements about any particular items; our son was 21 and equally supportive of us; and, as a result everything went like clockwork.

There was no better way to celebrate our mutually-agreed upon divorce settlement than to head to the Green Parrot Bar for Long-Island Iced Teas before her departure for New York. And celebrate we did.

However, I was quick to remind her that even on the very day of our divorce, I got into her pants! Ha!

NOTE: The article below originally appeared in the Oct. 31 – Nov. 13, 1991 issue of Solares Hill, Key West. Though written in the early 1990s, they have significances just as important today as when originally written.

Destination: Fort Jefferson

(In Search of Nirvana)

WHEN you live in an area referred to as "The Smiling Islands," "Paradise," and "The Last Resort," where can you go to get away from job stress and the routine of daily life? I recently opted to fly by seaplane to historic Fort Jefferson in the Dry Tortugas – the most inaccessible National Monument and the largest masonry fortress in the western hemisphere.

Sixty-eight miles west of the southernmost tip of the Keys, the area is called "Dry" because of the lack of fresh water, and "Tortugas" for the huge sea turtles which were harvested for years but whose remaining population is now protected by law.

The flight over took 45 minutes. Mickey, the pilot from Key West Seaplane Service, joyously banked his craft at low altitudes around pilot whales, huge sea turtles, sharks, the shipwreck and treasure sites of Spanish galleons, and the shockingly clear azure waters around the Marquesas Islands.

In the early hours of the morning the horizon was a fine, barely discernible line in the distance. If Mickey had said we were flying upside down, and the sky was the water and the water the sky, only gravity would have provided the correct answer.

Then the fort appeared. The incongruity of a massive 12-million-brick structure with eight-foot thick walls rising 50 feet above the Gulf of Mexico gave me the feeling I had entered a time warp. With its half-mile circumference, the fort housed 350 gun turrets and was completely surrounded by a 30-foot-wide moat. The magnitude of the project is almost unfathomable when you consider the era in which it was constructed and the materials that had to be brought to the Dry Tortugas by ship.

A Fort, But No Fight

THE fort was built in the 1840s, when it was believed that whoever controlled the area waters here would control all vital sea traffic from the gulf of the Mississippi River around to and up the Atlantic Coast.

But it was destined to never serve its purpose. Instead, Fort Jefferson stands as an oddity, never fully completed because of the hurricanes, shifting foundation, malaria outbreaks and a military design which was outdated before it could be put to use.

During the Civil War, Fort Jefferson became a hell-hole for deserters. It also served as the prison for felons such as Dr. Samuel Mudd, who was convicted of being a conspirator because he treated the broken leg of President Lincoln's assassin, John Wilkes Booth. When the fort's doctor was ill with malaria, Dr. Mudd treated the patients and was later pardoned by President Andrew Johnson for his good work there. His descendants still fight to further clear his name.

A National Treasure

TODAY the fort, which is operated and maintained by the National Park Service, is an historical attraction and a home base for several marine research teams. It also offers a dozen campsites which are located near a small, sandy beach and wonderful snorkeling areas in the surrounding waters. Access to the island is by plane or boat. During my five-day stay I was the only camper there.

Twice daily I snorkeled around the fort's moat and to various coral heads offshore. The clear, aquarium-like waters were home to myriad colorful fish and coral formations. I took many photographs with one of those inexpensive cameras you just mail in when finished. Nurse sharks, rays, tarpon, barracuda, octopi, angelfish, tangs, parrotfish, yellowtail and innumerable smaller fish made the venture joyful, relaxing and fulfilling.

On two corners of this tiny island stand the remains of the coaling piers once used to refuel Navy vessels and last used in 1908. It was from this anchorage that the Battleship Maine departed for its fatal trip to Havana Harbor. The iron posts which supported the piers are crisscrossed beneath the surface creating a maze of passageways and narrow openings. These house colorful fan corals and fish, which range in size from the tiny, iridescent blue-and-yellow damsels to four-foot silvery-scaled tarpon.

The Tortugas are homes or stopping ground to an abundance of fauna. Birders can expect sooty terns, noddy terns, brown pelicans, palm warblers, plovers, kingfishers, Atlantic gulls and many others. The magnificent frigate birds have claimed a section of mangrove as a rookery, and the males can be seen filling their brilliant red pouches with air in courtship display. Feisty hermit crabs scramble along the sandy beaches. Live conchs are common in the shallow waters near the mangrove keys.

A Time To Reflect

SINCE I had come to Fort Jefferson to relax and meditate, I found myself comparing my life to the life that surrounded me at the fort.

How do people relate to the diversity in nature? We too are of various pigmentations and there are no two of us exactly alike. Some of us travel alone; others in groups – schools of mammals finding our way. Some prey upon others; some band together finding strength in numbers. Some die young; others are diseased and infirm while others live long lives on the scale of human time. And we wear our various colors too, superficially.

Do we, unlike life in the sea, create our anguish by not flowing with the flow? We ask so much of ourselves. We complicate where we could simplify. We grieve where we could accept; we cling instead of releasing. We wish rather than do. We resist when we could be free.

The morning of my departure I realized that "place" matters little. There is no Nirvana with magic answers. Magic can happen anywhere: in Central Park, in the mountains of Tibet, in the middle of a battlefield, the Buttes of Montana or at Fort Jefferson – but only when "thinking" dissipates and harmony is welcomed in – the natural emptying to receive. The challenge is to retain the peaceful state when re-emerging, to go forward and accept what each day brings as a gift, a lesson, an opportunity.

An Unlikely Departure

THE departure from Fort Jefferson was more than I could have imagined. Ten minutes before the flight was to leave, Mickey, the pilot, walked over to me and said, "There's been a change in plans. We have to escort a prisoner back to Key West."

Four days earlier a former mental patient left a half-way house and had stolen a waverunner from a Key West business in an attempt to run it the 90 miles to Cuba because he was sure Castro would approve of (and pay for) his trip to his homeland, Israel. Unfortunately he had headed South instead of West and ended up on Loggerhead Key, about four miles from Fort Jefferson.

A Coast Guard boat working on navigational buoys had rescued the man and brought him to the fort. He was dehydrated and severely sunburned.

For some reason he believed that if he could make it to Cuba, Fidel would fly him to Israel, his final destination. Born in Tel Aviv, he had become a naturalized American, been in and out of several "homes," and was talking about suicide if he couldn't get back to Israel.

Because of the prisoner's unpredictable and disoriented state of mind, he was duly handcuffed and led to the plane. Mickey issued me a Park Service belt; an inch-and-a-half-wide, quarter-inch-thick piece of tooled leather, with instructions for me to sit directly behind the prisoner, hold each end of the belt tightly in my hands, and to loop it around the man's neck to restrain him if he made any attempt to charge the pilot or exit the plane.

The worst part of the ordeal was just being in the same enclosed space with this man who had not bathed for at least four days and who had recently urinated in his pants. The stench was reminiscent of cow barns where the urine-soaked hay becomes so "ripe" you can hardly breathe.

The prisoner remained handcuffed and seat-belted throughout the flight, occasionally mumbling to himself and lightly banging his head against the window, often taking deep breaths and sighing as he exhaled. You couldn't help but feel pity for this man who was lost, confused and debilitated. Here was a grown man in his forties, imbalanced and desperate enough to steal a small pleasure craft to get to Cuba.

Seven On A Raft

I THOUGHT of the snorkeling trip out to the reef I had taken a couple of months earlier, during which time we came upon a makeshift raft of wooden crates and inner tubes with seven Cubans cramped aboard. They had fled their country in the middle of the night; casting their fates to the currents and finding refuge in the Keys eight days later, having traversed 12- to 18-foot swells while crossing the Gulf Stream. Other family members and friends had left on a separate raft that same night and were never heard from again.

So here we had one craft fleeing Cuba; another trying to get there. Was our prisoner any more deluded than the Cubans in their flight for freedom? Was the peace and freedom they sought to be found by crossing some body of water, some political boundary? Was the peace and solitude I sought to be found in the Dry Tortugas?

As we landed in the waters near Key West, A Florida Marine Patrol boat circled us. Representatives from the Key West Police Department, the U.S. Naturalization and Immigration Services, reporters and photographers from the Key West newspapers and curious onlookers had all gathered to view this mystery man, who had headed for Cuba, gotten lost and was being returned in handcuffs.

Because the prisoner never reached Cuba, the immigration official was relieved to turn him over to the police. After receiving medical treatment he was charged with grand theft and taken to the Monroe County jail.

Was there any difference between the disoriented prisoner, the Cubans and myself? No. Even though the answers lie within, the following statement is still true: "No man is an island unto himself."

Just like the fish and coral, we are all part of the universal oneness.

Dolphin Encounters

From the Journals of Major T. Benton

July 1, 1992 – Little Bahama Banks.

THIS is all very hard to take in. Three days ago the opportunity suddenly presented itself for me to join ten others for the Wild Dolphin Project, a week's trip aboard the Stenella, a 62' catamaran research vessel which annually studies spotted dolphins in the Bahamas. This is the eighth year of a planned 20-year research project.

We have an extremely harmonious crew of eleven individuals aboard. Besides me, there's Leonard, so obviously talented as a photographer and willing to help and share, plus a natural bit of deserved ego thrown in. Mike the body-builder, has gotten out of a bad relationship and is looking for some peace in his life. Jeff, the quiet one, is obviously an extremely nice person with a genuine laugh and love for living. Katherine is everybody's mom who is out to save the planet. And Heather, Katherine's 30 year-old daughter from L.A. who is floundering in her search for life's meaning. Then there's the crew: Denise, quick, witty, intelligent, genuine; Laura, Denise's assistant and my best friend; big Bill, the mate, quiet, smart, silently committed, everybody's friend; Capt. Dan, in his own world; and, lastly, Diane, the cook, but much more than that, a bit of a bleeding heart but very well-intentioned, genuinely sweet and loving, plus unpretentiously classy and a helluva woman/person. It's obvious we will all get along famously. And, according to Denise, our good vibes as a group usually means a lot of positive encounters with dolphins, something she feels they can sense.

Not only this trip, but the last six to seven months are hard for me to take in. Since separating from a 26 year marriage last November, doors keep opening for me, wider and wider. More interesting people keep coming into my life, particularly females, which, for whatever reason, has always been the case for me. Laura has grown to be the love of my life, in a best-friend kind of way. What a refreshing gift she is to the world, and the Universe—a dolphin masquerading as a human!

I have no idea what this all means. I feel blessed in so many ways, as if I've been given a gift to share with everyone I contact. For some reason people respond to me. Somehow I uplift their spirits, give them renewed hope and strength, make them smile, be more at peace, encouraged, and appreciative of themselves—giving them self-confidence. Maybe it's what I've been learning from the dolphins and I'm just passing it on. Dolphins, dolphins, dolphins! What's the magic? Why do dolphins raise such various responses from everyone whenever they are mentioned? They are surely more than a metaphor. I do come away from being around them feeling both mellow and energized. Something has occurred within my consciousness which has had a profound positive effect on me and those with whom I come in contact.

Six of us rode in a taxi from Freeport to West End where we boarded the Stenella. West End could just as well be called Land's End. It's a desolate, has-been spit of land and marina reminiscent of something left remaining if a war had been fought here years ago. Not even quaint. On the ride out with our entertaining driver, Alfred Jones, we passed a road sign stating: "Undertakers Love Overtakers," which Alfred explained meant, "Slow de hell down mon, don follow so dom close, and don pass or do enytin tupid, or de undataker he hab you good!"

The water out here is beautiful: Deep blues and aquas with great visibility and a surprising variety of fish and other marine life. But also, much too much garbage and other marine debris floating everywhere—discarded light bulbs, five gallon plastic oil container, and miscellaneous junk. Still, it's very peaceful, colorful and mesmerizing. More and more I feel a closeness to the sea, as if it's my true home. Home again, home again, Home to the sea.

July 2, 1992

"AND they said you couldn't raise the dead," said Capt. Dan upon arising this morning. It's a hazy sunrise after a hazy sunset last night. I slept outside, just forward of the Bridge. A cool breeze kept lifting the edges of my light blanket to the point I eventually encased myself like a mummy to keep warm. This foreign sleeping location, out in the cool, moist night air, perhaps seven feet above the water's surface is probably as close as I've ever come to living in the dolphin's world. With the stars so clear overhead, my thoughts were filled with images from the book, A Friend in the Water, and, specifically, Dart, Natua, Captiva, Little Bit, Omega, and other dolphins I've encountered who have touched my life so meaningfully. They were ever-present as I realized I was only a terrestrial visitor to this alien watery world.

July 3, 1992

YESTERDAY afternoon I had an incredibly energizing, mesmerizing, peaceful, soul-searching, contemplative, spontaneous, unconditional love encounter in the water with ten spotted dolphins. The eye contact was indescribable and I was so "taken" by the experience of the moment that it's lucky I'm alive to write about it. Not only did I forget to regularly surface for air and felt like I swallowed a few gallons of seawater, but I was also so enraptured by the interaction that at one point I came up alongside one of the dolphins, both of us heading up for air, when I conked my head on the bottom of the Stenella. I

Dolphin Encounters

saw stars for a moment (almost blacking out), then still had to swim from under the boat and get to the surface for air!

I don't know what words to use to express the feelings of being eye-to-eye with dolphins, body-to-body, twisting, diving, spinning, playing games, watching a mother teaching her calf to catch fish from the sandy bottom, being playful, trusting and totally unconditional. When the thirty minute encounter ended, the games didn't. Captain Dan fired up the Stenella and all ten dolphins rode the bow wave of our boat for fifteen minutes. It was as if this was their reward and our gift to them for their coming in to be with us.

I slept well last night, totally in awe of the day's experience, lying there on deck in the night breeze with a full sky of stars overhead, listening to Peter Kater and Carlos Nakob with beautiful flute and piano music. In my own little world, with sweet thoughts of dolphins, how unbelievably fortunate I am to be here, feeling universal love for everyone, and seeing those dolphin eyes staring at me over and over again from only inches (3"-6"?) away. I kept getting the peaceful, ancient look from them; the mystery-of-the-ages stare; the all-encompassing "I am the Universe, You are the Universe; We are the Universe" feeling. Dolphins create the understanding within ourselves that says, "Yes, We are all connected—Mitakuye Oyasin."

There are rougher seas today, making it more difficult to write. Denise broke us up into two teams; team A and team B. This means each time dolphins are sighted, one team stays on board to keep a safe eye on the others and record pertinent information about the dolphins on hand, and then we switch whenever the next group of dolphins come along. Between encounters, one group rests while the other group keeps an eye out for dolphins and records various weather and scientific information in the log books.

July 4, 1992

JUST went through a squall. Winds and waves picked up dramatically, plus thin, vertical lightning strikes followed by reverberating rumblings of thunder. It was quite fun and a nice change from the norm, with great photo opportunities and cause for boisterous cheers from the crew! When the lightening got closer, we were smart enough to go inside where we watched the PBS Nature series film on dolphins. We also discussed the captivity issue for a couple of hours. It was a valuable exchange of thoughts, all boiling down to what hypocrites we all are! Laura, in her subtle say of stating issues and different viewpoints, was very convincing and caused several bleeding hearts to rethink their positions and "allow for other possibilities," to which they had previously limited themselves. It's difficult for me to realize I've only been employed in the dolphin "field" for less than nine months. I feel like dolphins have always been a part of me, perhaps in parallel lives or other lifetimes. I definitely recall as a child what powerful feelings would well up inside me when I sighted dolphins in the Chesapeake Bay and the ocean off Virginia Beach. Of course then everyone called them "porpoises."

July 5, 1992

YESTERDAY was a 4th to remember forever. It began at 7 A.M. with the sighting of five Atlantic bottlenose dolphins, followed by an exciting squall which ran us all inside for an hour, then four or five unreal encounters with spotted dolphins, two of the encounters lasting over an hour each. I felt totally honored to be accepted by them so unconditionally, especially by Hadley, a female foxy lady who gave me the "eye" and teased and played with me continually. We really had a thing going between us, and I even squawked through my snorkel to her that I loved her and thanked her for sharing her time and energy with me this unforgettable day.

Additionally, I found myself being the object of pursuit by a group of six dolphins who maneuvered me into position so that I was the "middle-man trailer" whereby three were on each side of me as they placed me slightly below them in the middle. I barely had to move my flippers as they drafted me along with them. It was unabashed acceptance and trust, something I consider a rare privilege afforded me at this "moment." I was so taken with what had occurred, and feeling so emotional about it, I got out of the water early to give the others more opportunity. I felt the dolphins had hogged me somewhat, plus I was totally overwhelmed by the experience.

The last dolphin encounter concluded around 8 P.M., and there were still dolphins everywhere, especially the extremely appealing youngsters. Each time Dan would move the Stenella they would all gather and ride the bow wave. Young ones as well as adults would repeatedly dive and jump totally out of the water on speed runs to reach the bow for a free ride. We topped off our July 4th celebration with watermelon margaritas, followed by a great dinner. Afterwards we all went forward of the Bridge and under a starlit sky listened to Denise, the leader of the Wild Dolphin Project, play guitar and delicately sing various folk songs, sea shanties, and requests from the rest of us. Just after midnight Denise stopped in the middle of a song and whispered, "Listen. Dolphins." We could hear them alongside the boat as they came up for a breath. Six spotted dolphins, as best we could tell, paid us a visit for almost thirty minutes. What an unbelievable cap to a fantastic 4th!

Our night/morning ended at 1:30 A.M. with Laura, Diane, Denise and I sleeping on the outside deck just forward of the Bridge, the spot I'd slept alone for each previous night. As I lay between Laura and Diane I couldn't get the grin off my face. I was, and still am so happy and thankful for all that's occurred on this trip. Listening to Denise play and sing last night was another privilege for me. What a day, what a day, what a day!

It's hard to believe we're nearing the end of another incredible day of natural beauty— water, sun, clouds, and social contacts among our group and with the dolphins. Everyone was dead tired today after yesterday's incredible encounters. We didn't see how we could ever again match the experiences of the previous 24 hours—yet we did match them and even exceeded them.

At one point today, five of us swam for over an hour with 21 spotted dolphins. The icing on today's cake was the mellowness and even more complete trust shown us by this group. Several of them continually rubbed their bodies against ours, with both dolphins and humans totally enjoying the rapport. Several individual dolphins showed particular fondness for one or more in our group. Laura and one female dolphin spent much time together playing games of twisting back and forth, side to side, over and under each other. On another occasion Laura was being escorted by 10 dolphins at once—4 on one side of her and 6 on the other. She also had an individual encounter with a male dolphin who showed her much attention as well.

I had a great time in the water with my own encounters but also just in observing everyone else. Katherine stayed with one young female dolphin for 15-20 minutes who twice tail-slapped her flukes only a few feet from Katherine's mask. But the behavior was not one of annoyance, but play, as it immediately rested on the surface and floated face to face with her.

Diane and Billy also had individual or small groups (2-3) to themselves with fantastic interaction displayed. Diane also rested on the surface for several minutes with one dolphin and exchanged eye contact continuously. Billy, who is a large individual and who we referred to as a "Tursiops" (Atlantic bottlenose dolphin) himself, had three dolphins with him constantly and had the most fun diving head first to the bottom, about 20 feet down, and remaining upside down while the three mimicked and circled round him.

The word for the day was tactile, tactile, tactile! Stub and Stubette, a male and female with dorsal fins shortened probably through interspecies tussles or possibly shark attacks, were especially tactile with everyone and gave me my first side-to-side touch with wild dolphins. It's still unbelievable to me that they are so trusting and inviting. They initiate the contact and certainly appear to want more and more of it. They definitely recognize Denise and hang around her all the time. They surely give her and the rest of us the distinct impression they want more physical contact, especially body rubs. Among themselves, the dolphins are constantly rubbing against each other with pec fins, dorsals, rostrums, and every other body part, including the entire body. We often saw rostrums placed onto genital areas of both males and females, by both males and females. Several were seen actually copulating, and there was constant body posturing.

Although they could have just taken off whenever they felt like it, they acted like they wanted a bow ride in return for all they had done for us. At one point during a later encounter today, it appeared that less than half the group of dolphins agreed to come over and interact, while the majority hung out together about a quarter mile away till it might be bow-riding time for all of them. It was as if they were willing to pay their dues for a bow ride later by choosing to send a few over to "entertain" us now. Actually, "interact" might be a better word choice than entertain.

Every time I'm around dolphins I feel myself opening more, allowing the possibilities, loving even more unconditionally; my awareness being expanded, my emotions more expressible, my connections and bonds to others stronger, more sincere and meaningful.

July 6, 1992

TRANSFORMATIONAL encounter #6,394! How the hell can I possibly come up with words to describe this morning's encounter? For perhaps 45 minutes to an hour I was alone with 13 dolphins. How can I tell the story? Where are the words? How can I explain what made me cry for an hour afterwards? Why I couldn't talk to anyone or answer their questions of what it was like?

Maybe rather than attempting to say what occurred chronologically, I'll just begin by saying what I'm feeling now—what I'm left with—for this lifetime and many more. I was wonderfully lost in another world. I had absolutely no conception or thought of anything other than what was occurring at the moment. Mesmerized doesn't even begin to describe it. The "message" didn't seem to be some attempt at understanding the "dolphinese" language or communication system, but a message about humans living together more productively and peacefully in everything—the old "we are all connected" syndrome. It was explained to me by someone on board, Katherine I believe, that there was special significance in their being 13 dolphins with me, having to do with 13 times a year women go through mensuration, and that 13 in a tarot card sense of thinking says something about there are neither lucky nor unlucky events which occur, but you create what happens. Joseph Campbell's "You are that mystery which you are seeking to find" comes to mind, or "Follow your bliss and doors will begin to open you never dreamed possible," along with Lin Yutang's "You never find yourself, you create yourself."

If I felt anything describable today it was the indescribable Tao—the emptying and filling, the giving and receiving, the going with the flow—no, not the going with the flow but being the flow, one in all, the Universe in the smallest imagining. Yes, there were the dolphin's antics to observe; games on/in the sand, rubbing, butting, body posturing, jaw popping/snapping, nips on various spots, pec touches, rostrum stimulation of genitals, hierarchy, cliques, pursuing fish, uncovering food sources hidden beneath the sand, much clicking, whistling, sonaring, squealing and squawking, and of course the eyes. You can never forget the wizened eyes. In other words, with total, unconditional acceptance of my being among them, the dolphins were just being dolphins. There was no fear, no worry, and no judgments being made.

Today I was a giver and receiver of unconditional trust and respect. Constant eye-to-eye contact always said more than any communicating could have dreamed of by the ordinary standards of sound or other body language. The rubs I was given by the sides of their bodies, dorsals, pecs, peduncles and flukes were only returned by my accepting them and not pulling away. I never felt any need to reach out to them or pursue them. They accepted me on their terms; I accepted them on theirs as well.

Again, I feel the message was not one of how we can interact with dolphins and learn to communicate with them (for they "talked" to me in their language and I to them in mine), but how we humans can communicate better with our own kind. Yes, there will be fights, misunderstandings, cliques, hierarchies, good loving, joy, political posturing, games to play, entanglements to work through, but we can be so much more successful at life and get done what absolutely must get done by being more open and receptive, more giving, more trusting, and definitely more unconditional in everything we do.

This in no way describes what happened to me personally this morning: not the love I felt; not the expansion within my soul; not the shutting off of the mind and the opening up within my heart; and surely not what I will carry with me from the experience on a day-to-day, in the moment, basis. The energized mellowness that I always sense from any dolphin interaction, grew by leaps and bounds this week.

Do I get emotional about this? Perhaps a little airy-fairy? You betcha! And do I apologize for that? No way! As Popeye said, "I yam what I yam." And as Henry Thoreau said, "If I am not I, who will be?" Everything I had heard about last night but had not yet experienced on this trip, especially the being sonared and being totally overcome emotionally, occurred this morning.

My group wasn't even scheduled to go out with the dolphins this morning. I had been up early and on watch from the bridge when I saw the dolphins coming in. When I notified the other team, they immediately got their gear and went into the water, which happened to be a little rough this morning. Katherine had just gulped down her morning coffee when she got the word, but quickly got into the water, perhaps too quickly. While swimming out to the pod of dolphins she got water into her snorkel several times, swallowed too much sea water and didn't feel well enough to continue. She came back to the boat and asked if I would like to take her place. I was in the water in a flash but wasn't sure where to head since the other members of her group had already made contact with the seven or eight dolphins that had arrived and split up into three small groups. I didn't want to interrupt their encounters so headed off to one side. That's when the other 13 dolphins appeared out of nowhere and took me into their pod.

When my time with them was over and the pod gathered about twenty yards ahead of me, took one long look back as if to say goodbye, and then disappeared from sight, that was the first time in almost an hour that the normal dimensions of time and space reentered my mind. I bobbed to the surface and looked around for the Stenella. I couldn't believe how far away I was from the boat; several hundred yards. The crew told me later they were keeping an eye on me and could see I was having a fantastic encounter and was in very good company with the dolphins. They also were the ones who told me I had been with the pod for almost an hour. I had absolutely no conception or time, distance, space, or anything else the entire time.

When I pulled myself up the ladder onto the boat, my emotions would not let me speak. I was totally choked up and everyone knew that. They started to ask questions, but then let me alone to work it out by myself. I went halfway down the starboard side of the boat, braced my feet against the rail, and stared out across the water. Tears continued to flow as the comprehension of what had occurred began to sink in. Diane, on her way from the bow to the stern, stopped momentarily behind me, gently massaged my neck and shoulders, and quietly said, "I'm so happy for you. I know what you're feeling and how overwhelming your experience was. It's something each of us have been so fortunate to experience at one time or another. Today was your day. The fact that Katherine returned to the boat early, which allowed you to go in, was another example of how everything happens exactly as it is supposed to happen. No plans, no expectations. Just let it be. This is what is. What teachers they are, huh? I love you Major. We all do, unconditionally. That's the beauty of the dolphins."

It was still hard to talk about to anyone. And everyone knew that and didn't ask me any more questions. They respected what had occurred. (I still find it extremely difficult to explain to anyone what I felt that day. And I still feel the emotions well-up inside me when I think about it. And, fortunately for me, I still shed joyous tears when I relive those moments. They will always be with me. Harmony is everywhere but is so ordinary that it is commonly missed. This morning's experience was, for me, extraordinarily ordinary: the Tao.

Major T Benton

Note: The following two articles originally appeared in the
April 16-29, 1992 issue of Solares Hill, Key West.

Reaching The Whales

Back and quickly! Out to sea again!
Go on, go on; wander the high seas.
    From *The Odyssey* by Homer

DOCKED alongside a pier at the Truman Annex, is the elegant yacht, Odyssey, a world-class, steel, motor-sailer, 93-feet long and weighing 98 tons. She was built in New Zealand in 1976 and can comfortably accommodate up to 14 people.

The Odyssey was under private ownership until recently, when a financially generous deal was made to turn her over to the Whale Conservation Institute. The WCI is a non-profit group about to embark on a four-year, around-the-world expedition as soon as it can raise the necessary funds.

Their accomplishments include 22 years of cetacean (or whale and dolphin) research data: the sampling and analysis of the world's largest collection of whale songs, the pioneering of several non-lethal marine mammal research techniques, and a world-wide education and conservation outreach program.

The Institute has also completed over 30 documentaries, plus it has provided assistance on two major motion pictures, "Star Trek—The Voyage Home" and "The Hunt for Red October." Their whale-song recordings have even reached outer space as part of the payload of the Voyager 1 and 2 spacecrafts. Two of their recordings, "Songs of the Humpback Whale," and "Whales Alive," have been big sellers, with the latter being nominated for a Grammy award.

Reaching The Whales

An Invitation From Pritam Singh

So what's the Odyssey doing in Key West? According to the Odyssey's Captain, Iain Kerr, "I have to be quite blunt and say it's because of Pritam Singh," a member of the Institute's board of directors.

Singh, the local developer, agreed to let the Odyssey have free dockage and electricity, and to help out the crew with their programs and other projects.

"For example," says Kerr, "a guy working for Pritam helped us with a piece of welding the other day for free. And Pritam made possible the Hot Tuna fundraising concert at the Reach Hotel in January."

According to Kerr, "Our connection with Pritam Singh began about four years ago. Pritam wanted to support programs with dolphins as an educational outreach. And his idea was to make it a far more vibrant environment for the dolphins and to be done in conjunction with the Dolphin Research Center (DRC) of Grassy Key.

"What actually happened was I was invited as a adjudicator type of thing, with Pritam Singh, the lawyers, John Paul Gouin (the Frenchman who owned DRC) and Mandy Rodriguez, who was running DRC along with his wife, Jayne. I was just sitting there and every now and then someone would ask me what I thought, and I would say this and that and this and that. Eventually Pritam asked, 'Who the hell are you?'

"I wasn't officially asked to be there, but had been asked to come along by Mandy. I had just come back from the Galapagos, had wild hair and everything, and I said, 'Well I do this and that with whales, etc.' I looked around and said 'Oops, sorry. I didn't mean to be taking over your meeting.' And Pritam said, 'No, no, this is my meeting. You just keep talking and I'll tell you when to stop.' And that was it."

The Odyssey crew views Key West as a community-oriented place, where people understand WCI's purposes and needs. They also compare the Keys to island communities where people live in harmony with the ocean, a place where people are more aware than most of the link between the oceans and land.

Dr. Payne Discovers A Song

THE president of the Whale Conservation Institute is Dr. Roger Payne, who discovered in the late '60s, along with his associate, Scott McVey, that the long, complex sounds made by humpback whales were actually songs. That started the "Save the Whales" movement (whose slogan was imitated in Key West by the popular T-shirts, "Save the Bales!"). The vinyl recording of whales songs that appeared in National Geographic still holds the number one spot for the largest single printing of any record to date.

Payne's achievements also include being knighted by Prince Bernhard of the Netherlands; a member of the International Whaling Commission; author of some 40 articles; and co-writer, presenter, and scientific advisor of a four-hour mini-series, "In the Company of Whales."

Current Mission Includes Developing Nations

THE Institute's current mission, tagged the "Odyssey Expedition," is to conduct and promote worldwide research, conservation, and education activities in support of cetaceans and their habitats. By providing information based on solid research, they hope to conquer the lack of understanding with which they believe many people view the wild world.

The expedition will also provide an opportunity for scientists and politicians in Third World developing countries to come on board, learn and participate. It will also utilize new film and media technologies to educate the project's own people.

The crew intends to dive deeply into the domain of the sperm whale, using sonar to study its behavior, foraging ecology, and the energetic costs associated with diving.

Some of the data to be collected will be baseline information on how insidious pollutants are dispersed in the ocean and into marine food chains. A continuous census of cetacean species encountered will enable the crew to learn more about population dynamics and dispersal.

The four-year around the world expedition will not only travel to the "hot spots" of known environmental degradation, but also to places people have never been. Many of them are out in the middle of the ocean where they'll simply stop and check for pollution, salinity levels, PCBs in the animals, and whatever else shows up.

The primary threat the whales face comes from toxic pollution, Kerr says, "If you look around at any animal, any species, you see that animals adapt to nature. What's the biggest thing about humans? Humans adapt nature to suit itself. And we've created compounds to which nature has no antidotes.

"We're dumping things into the oceans, and what happens is, in the case of PCBs, they dissolve in fat, not water, and they bio-amplify up the food chains, also producing the 'generation effect,' where the marine mammal mother, in her milk, passes along 30 percent of her toxic debt to the next generation."

Upgrade To A Full-Blown Research Vessel

THE Whale Conservation Institute is currently working to raise funds for the upgrade and operation of the Odyssey to a full-blown research vessel. She is a true blue water vessel, one that can spend extended periods of time offshore in all weather conditions. With her large pilot house, double-skinned hull, deep draft, sonar tube, crow's nest, and overall staunch construction, the crew would be hard-pressed to find a vessel more suited to their needs.

It would also be difficult to find a more able or dedicated crew. Besides Kerr as her captain and Dr. Payne as the on-board scientist, the Odyssey will also carry a engineer, cook, first mate, and deckhand, all earning only $100 a week during the expedition. Everyone pitches in wherever needed.

Kerr was born and raised in Scotland, earning an engineering degree in England where he then taught school. For years he has assisted Dr. Payne in Argentina studying right whales; he has also captained the 80-foot research vessel Siben on an international expedition off the coasts of North, Central and South America, logging over 25,000 miles at sea.

The engineer, Bob Wallace, has been with the Odyssey five years and knows the vessel "like a baby." Englishman Kit Rogers, the 24-year-old first mate, has a bio-chemistry degree from Oxford and has captained research boats in the Azores studying whales. Canadian John Atkinson is a poet and writer of children's books whom the group can send anywhere to represent them. Kerr describes Atkinson as "an over-talented consultant and representative whom we could not afford if we paid him what he's worth."

"With the Odyssey as our research platform we hope to become a 'voice from the sea'" says Kerr. "More than ever before, whales now have an acute significance as an indicator species, and perhaps as our ocean's canary in the coal mines."

Largest Brains On Earth

ALMOST everything about whales seems to be clouded in mystery. It is known, however, that they have the largest brains of any creature on earth, and many people feel their brains are more capable than our own.

In the February 26, 1990 issue of The New Yorker, writer Diane Ackerman quotes Roger Payne: "People often wonder just how intelligent whales really are. But I could argue that the human brain is the most unsuccessful adaptation ever to appear in the history of life on earth, because it threatens its owner with self-annihilation in fewer generations than any other organism. We may be the biggest flop that ever appeared on earth.

"Whales have an important lesson to teach us. They have a huge and complex brain but show no signs of threatening their own destruction. They haven't reproduced themselves into oblivion, they haven't destroyed the resources they depend upon, they haven't generated a giant hole in the ozone or changed the atmosphere so that the earth might end up with a runaway greenhouse effect."

For a while, whales came close to extinction and they became an engendered mystery. "It is an extremely important endangered mystery," says Payne, "because they may have the answer to how you can enjoy the fruits of this wonderful, magnificent calculator-computer-imaginer in your skull without threatening everything you hold dear. Whales seem to have done that."

Changes In Attitudes

TIM Kerr is greatly concerned with people's attitudes today. "People don't seem to realize, and this shocks me, that we're not drinking the water because it's got 'stuff' in it, and we're not jogging in Boston or L.A. because of the impurities in the air, and we're having to walk carefully on the beaches because of syringes, and garbage, and bottles, and all kinds of crap."

The Institute has observed how our lifestyles are being affected every day, and members feel it's not "if" we're going to make a change, but "when." Kerr Says, "We have to change our attitude towards the environment or else everything is going to be, in Jimmy Buffett's sort of ideology, 'swimming in a roped-off sea.' You can't go there, you can't be here."

Kerr believes we live in an information-bombarded society where it's almost impossible to filter out the positives. The type of change he's talking about is changing human perspectives and opinions. He says it can't happen overnight but will be the result of methodical persistency which will bring about a bridge between the ocean and humanity.

For him, technology is the key issue. "Not only is this the decade of the environment and high technology. This is also the decade of the environmentalists working with technology to help further their cause. It's crucial that science promotes public concern if we are to preserve the environment and these fascinating creatures (whales) for posterity."

Individual Efforts Are Imperative

KERR insists that no one should underestimate the value of an individual effort. He quotes Edmund burke, who said, "No one did worse than he who did nothing because he feared he could do so little."

Kerr uses the analogy of bees and honey to illustrate his point. People can walk into any store and see shelves of honey. Where did the honey come from? "From a million trips by a million bees carrying something so damn small we can't even see it. Yet look what their combined individual efforts produced."

Another example Kerr uses is beer cans. If the 40,000 or so people in Key West on any given day saves one beer can each, that would be 280,000 cans a week being recycled in this one spot.

The same analogy appears true for the support of the "Odyssey Expedition." Kerr says that if someone comes up and gives him one dollar for his program he'll be flattered and impressed, because if everybody in Key West did the same thing they would have 30- or 40- or 50-thousand dollars.

WHALE

Back To The Future

ROGER Payne hopes the work on the Odyssey will restore the balance of an earlier time. "At the beginning of time," he says, "we all had the right kind of wonder and reverence for whales. It got lost. And in that moment we not only lost something beautiful but something vital to our understanding of nature and our place in it."

From the same April 16-29, 1992 issue
of Solares Hill, Key West.

The Unknown Singh

AFTER a few years of tough press which focused on Pritam Singh's once-crumbling finances, the Truman Annex developer is beginning to receive favorable attention from the media again. In late January, the Miami Herald referred to him as a "survivor." It appears he has also earned the respect of area businessmen and politicians who seem to realize that he does, in fact, have the energy, willpower and business savvy to stick with the Truman Annex project through extremely tough financial times.

This interview with Singh, who practices the Sikh religion, took place recently in his office in the Truman Annex Management Co. The talk was about whales and the environment.

MAJOR BENTON: What is your association with the Whale Conservation Institute?

PRITHAM SINGH: I've been involved with them for, I think, four years. I'm actively involved in the affairs of the Institute, almost on a daily basis – dealing with various issues going on, including the direction of where the Institute goes, the philosophy of the Institute, and how we deal with the problems facing the environment. The Institute, of course, is involved with marine mammals, particularly whales and dolphins. I'm interested because I think we face an enormous threat to the environment, and this is one aspect of it; dealing with the research and understanding of marine mammals. One reason I got interested in the Institute is not only because I got involved with helping its direction, but also with going out and having interaction with marine mammals. I've become very close friends with Iain Kerr, the captain of the Odyssey (the Institute's research vessel), as well as the rest of the crew."

MB: The Nature Conservancy has an office in this building. Is this something you also participate in or help with in some fashion?

PS: Well, I gave them a bargain lease so they could get it for half the normal price. Within what I do, in my own job, I try very hard to be responsible by doing things like giving them access. I also give the Department of Community Affairs their space for a discount. You know this project area right here (Truman Annex) was the biggest industrial waste dump in the Florida Keys when I bought it. And now, it's the single best, environmentally sound real estate development in the Florida Keys.

We have a whole set of rules here which we voluntarily agreed to in terms of what we do with waste-water-runoff, etc., that no one else in the Florida Keys has agreed to or does. So not only have we cleaned up a huge amount of toxic waste on the site, but also, in terms of the water runoff that goes into the ocean here, it's very clean.

MB: Is this a side of Pritam Singh that most people in Key West know about?

PS: Nah (with a laugh), I don't think so. I've kept this pretty much to myself.

MB: Is this something personal that you felt you wanted to take part in?

PS: Well, I've always been interested in doing what I think is right. To express it in the terms of the way the Sikhs would put it, I want to be going "towards the Light, and away from the Darkness." Darkness I think is defined as ignorance, non-caring, greed and avarice. Going towards the Light would be just the opposite: caring about the world, compassion, kindness. So each day each of us has choices, and many times we make the wrong choices. As much as possible I'd like to make the right choices.

My public involvement within the community has primarily been my involvement with the Truman Annex development project: economics, aesthetics, etc., which I think is important. But just as important to me, and something I spend a huge amount of my time on, are these other issues. I think these environmental and ecological issues that face us are essentially the crucible that is going to change the way we see the world.

MB: Glancing at your bookshelves, I notice mostly titles like *Biospheric Politics*, *Gaia Consciousness*, and other environmental subjects. Is this your personal library?

PS: Yes. This is where I spend my time. This is what I'm interested in.

MB: You have an office downstairs as well as this one upstairs?

PS: The one downstairs is my business office. This is my real office. This one isn't the one I have to go to. This is the one I want to go to.

MB: From your perspective, is there anything in particular about the Whale Conservation Institute and the Odyssey Expedition that you would like to emphasize?

PS: Yes. They have a very unique program which they have devised, and I don't know how many people are aware of it yet. They're offering a program whereby donors in the $10,000 range can actually participate in the project, staying on board the Odyssey for ten days, and traveling to places they could not otherwise go, observing wildlife which is still in a state as close to Eden as imaginable – unusual and exceptional.

Like, for instance, the Galapagos Islands. And there are even parts of the Galapagos Islands that only they can go to. So you can literally be involved with this group in a way that allows you to go to places that are extraordinary, and to be involved in interacting with these creatures in a way that you otherwise couldn't. Plus you get to see first-hand precisely what your donation is paying for.

The Unknown Singh

MB: What incidents stand out for you as a supporter?

PS: Ask Iain (Captain Kerr) to show you the picture of him underwater looking up at 200 hammerhead sharks. And he's been swimming with sperm whales, pods of sperm whales, which are enormous mammals. Pretty courageous stuff! So I think you have a group here that goes into very special areas.

You know one of the biggest things that changed people's consciousness about animals and the natural world was when we realized that whales sing. Because that meant we all of a sudden realized that those creatures – other than human beings – have consciousness. It wasn't just mechanistic singing; it wasn't just a bird tweeting. Here was real intelligence. And Iain is like the guy in Star Trek, Captain Picard, who's a friend of ours. Captain Picard chases alien intelligence. And that's what Iain does. He does! And that's pretty incredible. This really is an extraordinary group of people, and I support them because I believe that.

Pritham Singh

April 23, 1982: Keys secede from Union, create Conch Republic

"By establishing that border, they have declared us a foreign nation," Wardlow said. The federal government soon removed the checkpoint, but the idea of the "Conch Republic" lives on. The Keys celebrates its Independence Day each year on this date. The "Conch Republic" flag can be found for sale in many forms. Souvenir passports are issued. And the Republic has spoken out in protest several times regarding various issues in the Keys since 1982.

Florida Keys 'Secede'

'The Conch Republic' Demands Removal of B(

KEY WEST (AP) — Mayor-cum-Prime Minister Dennis Wardlow raised the brightly colored banner of "The Conch Republic" in a properly eccentric noon ceremony yesterday that marked the Florida Keys' "secession" from the Union.

The Conch Republic will live, at least in the hearts and minds of the region's 40,000 residents, until the U.S. Border Patrol removes a controversial roadblock or the U.S. government sends a million dollars in "foreign aid."

A party atmosphere prevailed as Wardlow declared himself prime minister and "cabinet" members introduced themselves and talked of minting "bubba bucks" for currency. Wardlow joked that the self-proclaimed new nation was entering into "a vocal-shot" war with the United States, then will apply for foreign aid.

Some residents carried signs such as "Remember The Aloe" and "Welcome to the Third World," while others blew into conch shells. "Conch" is the term native Key Westers reserve for themselves, and the "bubba system"

is the island's fiercely protective network of cronyism.

However, a U.S. flag still flew within sight of the throng at Mallory Square, a dockside area where locals and tourists go each evening to watch sunsets.

The conchs are rebelling about the latest in a series of "hostile" actions by the U.S. government — a Border Patrol roadblock set up to snare illegal aliens and drugs believed to be smuggled into the country in the chain of myriad Keys. During the roadblock's first day last Sunday, traffic was backed up 19 miles at the "border" between the mainland and the Keys.

The Chamber of Commerce reports that hotels have taken hundreds of cancellations by mainlanders who don't want to end their weekend trapped in another checkpoint traffic jam.

While a federal judge in Miami on Thursday declined to order the roadblock halted, the Border Patrol does plan to relax the questioning of motorists and searches of cars.

"This is only partly humorous. There's a great deal of anger in this town," said Townsend Kiefer, a writer and civic activist who has

Florida Keys "Secede"

from U.S.

order Patrol Roadblock

been named minister of foreign affairs in the fledgling government.

"By establishing that border, they have declared us a foreign nation," Wardlow said. "Of course I'm serious. We're tired of getting kicked around. We're tired of the U.S. government picking on little Key West."

By Thursday, the roadblock, just south of Florida City, had netted 34 illegal aliens, 150 pounds of marijuana and three grams of cocaine.

Wardlow suggested that the Border Patrol would catch more illegal aliens and drugs by setting up on I-95 in Dade or Broward counties or along I-4 near Disney World in Central Florida.

Ironically, Key West was the only Florida city that remained in the Union during the Civil War. Then, the Union forces used Key West's harbor to avoid Confederate blockades.

"The only way to join back with the United States is by a peace treaty, that being the removal of the border up at Florida City," Wardlow said.

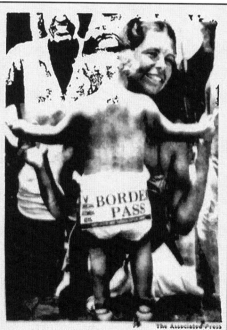

Sean Powell joins Key West protest

Major T Benton

A Variety of Additional Photos for Your Enjoyment

BIKES ON THE BEACH

Hemingway Look-Alikes, Key West

Hemingway's Studio and writing desk

A Variety of Additional Photos for Your Enjoyment

Hurricane in the Keys

Key West and Florida

A Variety of Additional Photos for Your Enjoyment

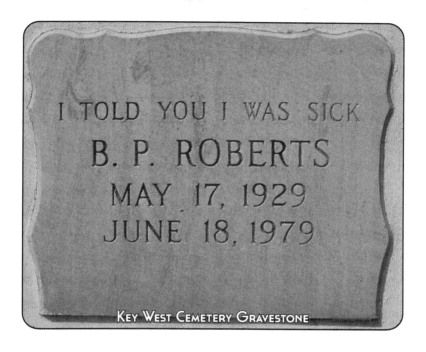

Key West Cemetery Gravestone

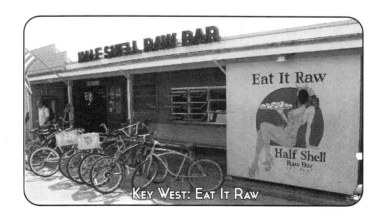

Key West: Eat It Raw

Key West Fishing

Key West - Sloppy Joe's Bar

A Variety of Additional Photos for Your Enjoyment

Mallory Square Monarch X

Mangrove Kayaking

Major T Benton

Overseas Highway

Pirate Dog

A Variety of Additional Photos for Your Enjoyment

POLYDACTYL CAT AT HEMINGWAY HOUSE

NEW YEAR'S EVE WOMAN IN RED SLIPPER

Snorkelling off Fort Jefferson

Southernmost Point at Key West

A Variety of Additional Photos for Your Enjoyment

Truman Little White House

The Buck Stops Here---Truman Desk

Tiger In The Woods Golf Tournament

A Variety of Additional Photos for Your Enjoyment

Major T Benton

Epilogue by the Author

Epilogue by the Author

I WAS fortunate to have lived in the Florida Keys for ten years, five in the Marathon area (Grassy Key), 1990-1995, and five more in Key West itself, 2000-2005, during which time I collected most of the 200 examples in this book. Most of the "BONUS" sections also came from experiences during those years. Since the writing here is non-fiction, you can also consider this material within the historical events of the time.

There is no other place in the world like Key West. Imagine 25,000+ people living on a two-mile by three-mile island at the Southernmost Point in the Continental United States. Beyond the fun, craziness and party atmosphere there also lurks a Key West that is a remarkably creative, cosmopolitan city whose scope includes most anything you would find in a much larger city; and one that encompasses tolerance, and the welcoming of people of varying nationalities, religions, abilities, sexual preferences, backgrounds, educations, politics, and experiences.

Yes, Key West may be a tourist town with a drinking problem, as some say, or a drinking town with a tourist problem according to others. Fortunately this little city offers a lot more than the partying. Many locals love to snorkel the coral reef, participate in the world-class fishing, visit the Dry Tortugas Islands, observe the large populations of wild dolphins, enjoy the beaches and parks, and going on eco-tours to visit the "backcountry" areas around Key West.

Art, culture and history abound in the Florida Keys. Key West is considered one of America's finest artistic communities with something to offer for everyone. There are exceptional art teachers, locally owned and operated galleries offering high-quality works, and a very supportive community of artists who make Key West proud. Yet, be wary of non-locally painted works of art and art-related objects with questionable provenances. Similar to many of the t-shirt sellers, if you are not careful, you just might get ripped off.

Whether you visit or live here, choose from a long list of things to do, slow your usual pace, and walk or bicycle around the beautiful historic districts. Absorb the multitude of opportunities to learn about Ernest Hemingway, the Shipwreck Historeum Museum, Audubon House, the Mel Fisher Maritime Museum, East Martello Tower, Lighthouse Museum and the Customs House Museum, as well as others. Check out the locally owned and operated book stores, the terrific Monroe County Library and the variety of locations for classical music, plays, and any number of other educational opportunities.

Take in the Tropic Cinema, South Florida's only non-profit multiplex cinema screening first-run indie, foreign and documentary films. Check out the Waterfront Playhouse, Red Barn Theater and other offerings too numerous to mention.

Most of all get to know the locals. They are amazingly friendly and helpful, providing insights and information you can't get anyplace else. It's a great place to be, but a hard place to leave. Something in the Gulf Stream air lulls you into a most pleasant atmosphere. Just do it!

And, finally, in case you were curious, I have some Good news: All 54 Cats at Ernest Hemingway's Key West home survived Hurricane Irma, the last major hurricane to hit the Keys!

About the Author

MAJOR T. Benton writes environmental, human interest, personal journals, natural history and other non-fiction from travels, research and experiences. He lived in the Florida Keys for 10 years, during which time he was:

- Caretaker of a private property on Grassy Key, just north of Marathon.
- Bellman, PBX Operator, Security Night Manager, Manager-On-Duty, Facility Manager of the "Dolphin Connection," and Marina Manager (not all at the same time) at Hawk's Cay Resort & Marina, Duck Key, Marathon.
- Researched Spotted Dolphins in the Bahamas as part of the Wild Dolphin Project.
- Island Administrator, Pigeon Key Foundation, Marathon, Florida.
- Security Manager, Truman Annex Master Property Owner's Association, Key West.
- Adjunct Professor of English at the College of the Florida Keys on Stock Island.
- Writer and Artist

Other life experiences include:

1. Captain, U. S. Marine Corps and Vietnam Veteran.
2. English Instructor, University of Maine, Orono and Augusta; Middle Tennessee State University, Murfreesboro; and, Wilbraham & Monson Academy in Massachusetts.
3. Reservations Manager, St. Croix-By-The-Sea Hotel, St. Croix, U.S. Virgin Islands.
4. Director of Laughing Brook Education Center and Wildlife

Sanctuary, and Moose Hill Wildlife Sanctuary for the Massachusetts Audubon Society.
5. Roustabout with the Clyde Beatty/Cole Brothers Circus.
6. Canoed the Allagash Wilderness Waterway in Maine.
7. Travelled to Ajawaan Lake in Prince Albert National Park in Saskatchewan, Canada, researching the life and writings of Archie Grey Owl.
8. Co-produced and published *MajorSigns*, a quarterly journal to inspire creativity and networking, which was distributed to subscribers in 36 states and 6 foreign countries.
9. Co-wrote *The Wisdom of Dolphins*, published in January, 2000, by Sourcebooks, Inc., Naperville, IL. This book was nominated for a Virginia Literary Award from the Virginia Center for the Book at the Library of Virginia.
10. Executive Director of the Virginia Zoological Society, Norfolk.
11. Conservation Officer and Chief Ranger of Hungry Mother State Park, in Marion, Virginia, after completing the Cardinal Criminal Justice Academy in Salem, Virginia.
12. Owner/Artist, Reese-Benton Gallery, Silver City, New Mexico.
13. Retired to México
14. Author of *An Analysis and Summary of Humor in the Writings of Henry David Thoreau: Who Was a Funny, Funny Man*, published in April, 2020, by Ajijic Books Publishing and available on Amazon, and *Pieces of My Puzzle: Selected Writings from a Reputable Vagabond*, May, 2020, also from Ajijic Books Publishing and on Amazon.com.
15. After every negative experience in my life - something more positive has resulted. Now I find myself getting really excited when something negative happens, so curious about what is coming next. I'm in no hurry to die, but when my time comes I can't wait to find out what happens!

Major T Benton

Made in the USA
Columbia, SC
06 September 2022